Worldwatch Paper 85

The Changing World Food Prospect: The Nineties and Beyond

Lester R. Brown

October 1988

The Worldwatch Institute is an independent, nonprofit research organization created to analyze and to focus attention on global problems. Directed by Lester R. Brown, Worldwatch is funded by private foundations and United Nations organizations. Worldwatch papers are written for a worldwide audience of decision makers, scholars, and the general public.

The Changing
World Food Prospect:
The Nineties and Beyond

Lester R. Brown

Worldwatch Paper 85
October 1988

© Worldwatch Institute, 1988
Library of Congress Catalog Card Number 88-51287
ISBN 0-916468-86-0

Table of Contents

Introduction

When the 1987 harvest began, world grain stocks totaled a record 459 million tons, enough to feed the world for 101 days. When the 1989 harvest begins, we estimate that these "carryover" stocks will drop to 54 days of consumption, lower even than the 57 days at the beginning of 1973 when grain prices doubled. During a brief two years, world reserves of grain—which account for half of all human caloric intake when consumed directly and part of the remainder in the form of meat, milk, cheese, butter, and eggs—will have dropped from the highest level ever to the lowest since the years immediately following World War II.[1]

Stocks have declined precipitously because food demand has continued its population-driven rise while production has fallen at a record rate. In 1987, a monsoon failure in India contributed to an 85-million-ton drop in world output. In 1988, drought-reduced harvests in the United States, Canada, and China reduced world grain output a further 76 million tons.[2]

The drought that afflicted the United States in 1988 is by many criteria the most severe on record—so severe that domestic grain production is projected to fall below consumption for perhaps the first time ever. North America, which furnishes most of the world's wheat and feed grain exports, was able to maintain exports in 1988 only by selling its carryover stocks. Another severe drought in 1989 would reduce exports to a trickle, creating a world food emergency.[3]

I am grateful to John Young for helping with research and analysis, to Reah Janise Kauffman and Susan Norris for production assistance, and to my colleagues Christopher Flavin and Sandra Postel for their thoughtful review comments.

The central question raised by this overnight depletion of world grain reserves is, What are the odds that North America will experience another severe drought in 1989? Are the three drought-reduced harvests of 1980, 1983, and 1988 simply reruns of the types of droughts that occurred in the thirties, or do they foreshadow an agricultural future in a world where summers in mid-continental North America will be far hotter? No one knows.

Drought can be caused by below-normal rainfall, by above-normal temperatures (which increase evaporation), or both, as was the case in 1988. Record-high temperatures in key U.S. agricultural areas during the summer of 1988 contributed to the reduced harvest. This record-setting summer cannot be conclusively linked to the long-projected global warming, but both the reduced rainfall and higher temperatures in the North American agricultural heartland are consistent with projected changes in climate associated with the buildup of greenhouse gases. Many meteorologists believe it is likely that the warming is now underway. They point out that the four warmest years during the last century have been in the eighties and that 1988 promises to be the warmest yet. If the warming is underway, droughts and heat waves will occur with increasing frequency, making it more difficult to rebuild stocks once they are depleted.[4]

In addition to the drought-reduced harvests, the growth of world food production appears to be losing momentum. Between 1950 and 1984, world grain output climbed from 624 million tons to 1,645 million tons, a prodigious 2.6-fold gain that raised per capita grain production by 40 percent. Since then, per capita output has declined each year, falling 14 percent over the last four years.[5]

The seeds for this slowdown were sown many years ago. During the fifties and sixties, the world's farmers had little difficulty keeping up with an unprecedented growth in food demand, but as the seventies began, the growth in output slowed and food supplies tightened. This deteriorating situation was brought into sharp focus by the decision of the Soviet Union to offset its 1972 crop shortfall by massive grain imports. Almost overnight, grain prices doubled. They remained high for several years and, as a result, production surged ahead. By the

"If the U.S. grain output produced
with unsustainable use of soil and water
is subtracted from the world total, the
surpluses of the eighties disappear."

early eighties, the alliterative phrase "a world awash in grain" was frequently used to describe the world grain market. Carryover stocks reached record levels, severely depressing crop prices.[6]

7

Even as reports of the huge surpluses were dominating the news during the early and mid-eighties, there were signs that some of the production gains came from overplowing and overpumping. Plowing highly erodible land was causing heavy soil losses and overpumping underground water for irrigation was lowering water tables.

In effect, we are feeding ourselves at the expense of our children. By definition, farmers can overplow and overpump only in the short run. For many farmers, the short run is drawing to a close.[7] This is leading to agricultural retrenchment, as farmers pull back from the excesses of the seventies. No one knows how much of the world's food output is unsustainable, but one can get an idea by looking at some examples from the United States. Under the Conservation Reserve Program, the U.S. Department of Agriculture is taking 11 percent of the country's cropland out of production, converting it to grassland or woodland, because it is too erodible to sustain continuous cropping. Irrigated area has shrunk 11 percent since 1978. Even so, the USDA reports that water tables are still falling by six inches to four feet per year beneath one-fourth of U.S. irrigated cropland, suggesting that further shrinkage is in prospect.[8]

If the U.S. grain output produced with this unsustainable use of soil and water is subtracted from total world output, the surpluses of the eighties disappear. If enough data were available on soil erosion and falling water tables to extend this calculation to the rest of the world, it undoubtedly would show that sustainable world food output is now running well below consumption.[9]

Depressed farm prices during the eighties have clearly slowed investment in agriculture, but other forces are shaping the world food prospect. For instance, the backlog of unused agricultural technologies that farmers can draw upon in some countries is dwindling, making it more difficult for them to maintain the rapid output growth of recent decades.

But beyond these economic and technological influences, the future of agriculture is being shaped increasingly by environmental trends and resource constraints. Prominent among these are the continual loss of topsoil from croplands, the conversion of cropland to nonfarm uses, the waterlogging and salting of irrigation systems, falling water tables, the diversion of irrigation water to nonfarm uses, and now the possible adverse effects of climate change.

In addition, demographic trends are making it ever more difficult to achieve a satisfactory balance between food and people. The annual addition to world population, estimated at 88 million in 1988, is projected to reach 91 million in the early nineties. By the end of the decade, there will be nearly a billion more people to feed. In the two regions with the fastest population growth, Africa and Latin America, per capita grain production is falling. If action is not taken soon to reverse these declines, hunger and malnutrition will spread, and eventually food consumption for some will fall below the survival level.[10]

Production Trends

The enormous growth in world grain output between 1950 and 1984 had no precedent. Never before had the world witnessed such an increase in food production within one generation. But can this rate be sustained indefinitely? Is an encore possible?

The last four years may help answer these questions. After increasing only slightly in 1985 and 1986, global grain production fell sharply in 1987 and again in 1988. (See Figure 1.) Measured in per capita terms, it fell in each of these four years.[11]

During the mid-eighties, grain production has plateaued in some of the world's most populous countries, including India, China, Indonesia, and Mexico. India more than tripled its wheat harvest between 1965, when the Green Revolution was launched, and 1983, sharply boosting total grain output. Since then its grain production has not increased at all.[12]

Million
Metric Tons

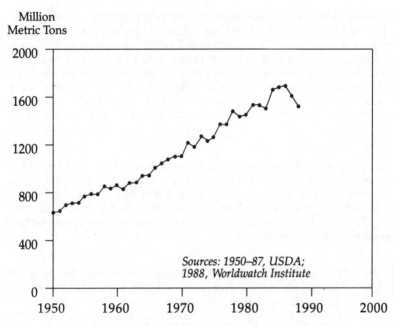

Sources: 1950–87, USDA;
1988, Worldwatch Institute

Figure 1: World Grain Production, 1950–88

China may illustrate the leveling off even more dramatically. The economic reforms that quickly led to exploitation of a large backlog of unused technologies boosted grain production by nearly half between 1976 and 1984, an impressive achievement by any standard. Since then, China's output has actually fallen slightly. Beijing's official goal early in 1988 was to regain the record level attained in 1984. An increase in grain procurement prices for the 1988 crop notwithstanding, China's planners announced in mid-June—well before the dimensions of this year's drought were apparent—that they would not achieve that goal. For the fourth year in a row, China failed to make it back to the peak production level of 1984.[13]

Indonesia doubled its grain harvest, consisting almost entirely of rice, between 1970 and 1984. Since then, output has leveled off. The only major rice-producing country situated astride the equator, Indonesia is retrenching geographically. Its resettlement program, designed to alleviate land hunger by moving people from densely populated Java to the outer islands, has been widely judged a failure and has come to a near halt. In contrast to Java's rich volcanic soils, those of the outer islands quickly deteriorate once the dense rain forest is cleared for farming.[14]

Mexico, where the Green Revolution originated, boosted its grain harvest four-fold between 1950 and 1984. There, too, production has stagnated, largely because the area in grain has declined one-tenth during the eighties. This shrinkage, as degraded cropland is abandoned and other cropland is converted to nonfarm uses, is offsetting the gains in yield per hectare.[15]

At the regional level, per capita production trends are beginning to diverge. During the fifties and sixties, grain production exceeded population growth on every continent; diets improved almost everywhere. Beginning in the seventies, however, production in Africa fell behind population growth, leading to a decline in production per person of roughly one-tenth. During the eighties, Africa has been joined by Latin America, whose decline dates to 1982, the year in which the debt crisis began.[16]

The food prospect for China is of special concern, not merely because it is the world's largest food consumer, but because its planners may be greatly overestimating its future gains in food production. Although planners project a 130-million-ton increase in grain production by the end of the century, or roughly 35 percent, there is reason to wonder if this goal is achievable. The recent experience of three other countries in East Asia with similar population-land ratios, and which have undergone rapid industrial development comparable to that now underway in China, raise questions as to whether this will be possible.[17]

"China's food planners may be
greatly overestimating future
gains in production."

In Japan, Taiwan, and South Korea, grain production has been declining for many years. In each of the three, the historical peak came during the 11-year-span between 1967 and 1978. From their respective peaks, production has declined more than one-fourth in Japan, by one-fifth in Taiwan, and by one-sixth in South Korea. (See Table 1.)

With a small area of cropland per person, it becomes difficult to boost output per worker in agriculture as fast as in industry. The rapid rise in labor productivity and income in the industrial sector pulls workers out of agriculture. As a result, the area multiple-cropped—growing more than one crop per year in one field—begins to decline. In addition to siphoning labor out of agriculture, the nonfarm sector also draws land away from farmers. Record rates of industrialization lead to rapid growth in land for the construction of factories, warehouses, access roads and, as affluence rises, new housing. In each of these three countries, the decline in grain area was followed in a matter of years by a decline in grain production.

For densely populated countries that are industrializing rapidly the comparative advantage lies in industry, not in agriculture. As a result, these countries have all greatly increased their grain imports over the last decade or two—an obviously sensible policy. Although all three are largely self-sufficient in rice, they import most of their wheat and nearly all of their feed grains. In 1987 imports accounted for 71 percent of Japan's grain consumption, 72 percent of Taiwan's, and 59 percent of South Korea's.[18]

The experience of these three similar countries may explain why China is now having such difficulty boosting its grain production. Like its three East Asian neighbors, China is densely populated and has a small area of cropland per person, a rapid rate of industrial development, and a nonfarm sector that is pulling both labor and land away from agriculture. In addition, in China's water-scarce north, the nonfarm sector is diverting water from irrigation.[19]

China's grain area peaked in 1976, and its grain production in 1984. With grain yield per hectare already within 15 percent or so of that in Japan, achieving the yield increases that are needed to reach the

Table 1: The Relationship Between Declines in Grain Growing Area and Grain Production in Four East Asian Countries

Country	1950	Year of Historical Peak	1987	Change 1950 to Peak Year	Change Peak Year to 1987
				(percent)	
Japan					
Grain Area[1]	4,993	5,075 (1955)	2,570	+2	–49
Grain Prod.[2]	15,611	20,285 (1967)	14,557	+30	–28
South Korea					
Grain Area[1]	1,954	2,374 (1965)	1,509	+21	–36
Grain Prod.[2]	4,903	9,863 (1978)	8,242	+101	–16
Taiwan					
Grain Area[1]	803	860 (1974)	643	+16	–25
Grain Prod.[2]	1,959	3,807 (1976)	3,040	+94	–20
China					
Grain Area[1]	91,871	101,348 (1976)	92,007	+10	–9
Grain Prod.[2]	108,970	366,010 (1984)	360,210	+226	–2

[1]Thousand hectares.
[2]Thousand tons.

Source: U.S. Department of Agriculture, Economic Research Service, *World Grain Harvested Area, Production, and Yield 1950–87* (unpublished printout) (Washington, D.C.: 1988).

one-third increase planned by the year 2000 will not be easy. If China cannot restore a steady growth in output, it will need to aggressively expand its industrial exports in order to import grain.[20]

In 1988, China imported 5 percent of its grain, roughly 15 million tons. If China's efforts to expand grain output are no more successful than those of its three smaller neighbors, it might be importing a steadily growing share of its food as the nineties progress. If it were to import 15 percent of its needs by 1995, the amount would total 45 million tons—more than the 28 million tons now imported by Japan and the 24 million tons by the Soviet Union, the world's leading grain importers.[21]

Perhaps the best indicator of long-term shifts in food production relative to demand can be seen in the changing geographic pattern of world grain trade. (See Table 2.) In 1950, most of the grain in international trade flowed from North America to grain-deficit Western Europe. The rest of the world was essentially self-sufficient. That has changed dramatically in recent decades. Since 1950, North America has increased its grain exports more than five-fold, from 23 million tons to 119 million tons, emerging as the world's breadbasket.

Latin America has become a grain-deficit region in recent years, with net imports of roughly 11 million tons in 1988. Despite its vast land area, Brazil now regularly imports both wheat and feed grains. These imports by Brazil and those by Mexico, with its growing food deficit, plus several smaller countries more than offset exports from Argentina.[22]

Imports of grain into two other continents, Africa and Asia, are rising steadily, though for different reasons. Africa is trying to offset a two-decade decline in per capita production. Asia is importing more because of its rising prosperity and its decision to exploit its comparative advantage in industry.

Africa, a largely agrarian continent beset by environmental deterioration and a record population increase, has become heavily dependent on imported grain. The northern tier of countries—Egypt, Libya,

Table 2: World Grain Trade by Region, 1950–88[1]

	1950	1960	1970	1980	1988[2]
	(million metric tons)				
N. America	23	39	56	131	119
L. America	1	0	4	–10	–11
W. Europe	–22	–25	–30	–16	22
E. Eur/USSR	0	0	0	–46	–27
Africa	0	–2	–5	–15	–28
Asia	–6	–17	–37	–63	–89
Aust/NZ	3	6	12	19	14

[1]No sign indicates net exports, minus sign net imports.
[2]Estimates.

Sources: U.N. Food and Agriculture Organization, *FAO Production Yearbook* (Rome: various years); U.S. Department of Agriculture, Foreign Agricultural Service, *World Rice Reference Tables* (unpublished printout) (Washington, D.C.: June 1988); USDA, FAS, *World Wheat and Coarse Grains Reference Tables* (unpublished printout) (Washington, D.C.: June 1988).

Tunisia, Algeria, and Morocco—now import half of the grain they consume. Even with continental imports of an estimated 28 million tons in 1988, millions of people in Sub-Saharan Africa were left hungry and malnourished, some on the verge of starvation.[23]

In Asia, the combination of a small and shrinking cropland area per person and rising prosperity in many countries has made it the leading food importing region. Its purchases surpassed those of Europe during the mid-sixties, and all indications are that they will continue to rise during the nineties and beyond.

Eastern Europe and the Soviet Union, which were importing at record levels in the late seventies and early eighties, are slowly reducing their dependence on grain from outside. Whether they reach self-sufficiency will depend heavily on the success of Soviet agricultural reforms.

Western Europe is perhaps the most interesting regional story. In the early eighties, it ended two centuries of dependence on imported grain, a dependence that began with the industrial revolution and the exchange of manufactured goods for food and raw materials with the rest of the world. Steadily advancing farm technologies, farm support prices well above the world market level, and a population growth that is approaching zero have combined to push the region's net grain exports above those of Australia. Although Western European farmers may face some reductions in support prices as the costs of maintaining current levels soar, they still may be able to export more grain than Australia, which with its semi-arid climate will find it difficult to substantially increase its exports.

The principal determinant of whether food production per person is rising or declining in the various geographic regions is the differential rate of population growth. Where population growth is slowest, Western Europe, per capita food production is rising most rapidly. In the two regions where population growth is fastest, Africa and Latin America, it is declining.[24]

The effect of widely varying population growth rates on per capita production can be dramatically illustrated by comparing the trends in Western Europe and Africa since 1950. Over the past 38 years, total grain output in Western Europe has increased 2.6-fold, and in Africa 2.2-fold. As a result, in Western Europe, where population growth is negligible, per capita output has more than doubled. But in Africa, whose population expands at a record 3 percent annually, output per capita has been falling since peaking in 1967. These contrasting trends are evident in Figure 2.[25]

These diverging regional trends notwithstanding, world grain production increased substantially faster than population from 1950 through 1984, boosting per capita output from 246 kilograms to 345 kilograms. This 40-percent increase in the per capita output of cereals led to impressive improvement in diets in many countries, boosting consumption of livestock products. During the last two years, when world per capita production of grain was falling by nearly 14 percent, record

Kilograms

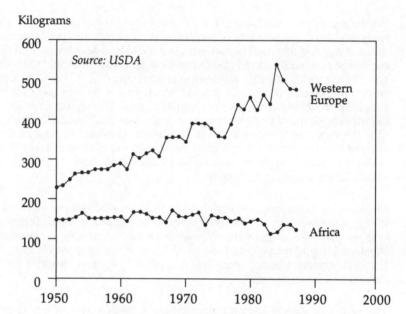

Figure 2: Per Capita Grain Production,
Western Europe and Africa, 1950–87

grain reserves permitted a drawdown of stocks to offset most of this decline, limiting the drop in consumption per person to 3 percent.[26]

Until recently, expanding food production was largely an economic concern, a matter of formulating agricultural price policies that would stimulate investment in agriculture. Today, rises in commodity support prices may simply result in the plowing of highly erodible land or the installation of more irrigation pumps where water tables are already falling. Given the soil and water constraints now facing farmers, it is not so surprising that world growth in production is slowing.

The overall loss of momentum in world grain output, exacerbated by the monsoon failure in India in 1987, the North American and Chinese droughts in 1988, and larger areas of cropland idled under U.S. grain supply management programs in both years, has depressed the world grain harvest by nearly 10 percent in two years. Record back-to-back declines have interrupted nearly four decades of steady growth in world grain output, one of the most predictable of global economic trends since World War II.

17

The Cropland Base

From the beginning of agriculture until the mid-twentieth century, most of the growth in world food output came from expanding cultivated area. Since 1950, a combination of the diminishing fertility of new land to plow and the availability of new technologies shifted the emphasis from plowing new land to raising land productivity. Roughly four-fifths of the growth in world food output since mid-century has come from this source.[27]

The world grain area increased some 24 percent between 1950 and 1981, when it reached an all-time high. (See Figure 3.) Since then, it has fallen some 7 percent. That the world's cropland area would expand when the world demand for food was expanding rapidly over those three decades is not surprising. What is surprising is that it has declined since then. This is due partly to the abandonment of eroded land, as in the Soviet Union, partly to the systematic retirement of such land under conservation programs, as in the United States, and partly to growing competition from nonfarm sources, a trend most evident in densely populated Asia.

From mid-century until 1981, there were two major surges in the world grain area. The first came in the early fifties, when the Soviets embarked on the "virgin lands" project. Between 1951 and 1956, they added some 40 million hectares, accounting for most of the steep growth in the world grain area shown in Figure 3.[28]

The second surge started when world grain prices doubled following the massive Soviet wheat purchase in 1972. Farmers throughout the

Million
Hectares

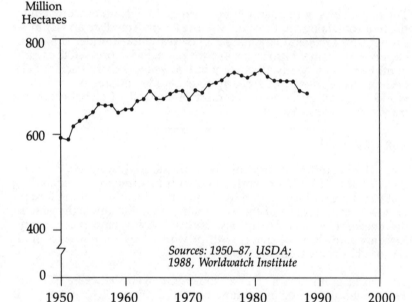

Figure 3: World Grain Harvested Area, 1950–88

world responded to the record prices by plowing more land. In the United States, they not only returned idled cropland to use, but they plowed millions of acres of highly erodible land. Between 1972 and 1976, the U.S. area in grain climbed some 24 percent. But, soil erosion increased as well. By 1977, farmers were losing an estimated six tons of soil for every ton of grain they produced.[29]

Meanwhile the Soviet Union, embarrassed by its 1972 crop failure, expanded its area in grain some 7 percent. By 1977, it had reached an all-time high. But erosion of soil by both wind and water also increased. Although detailed data on soil loss are not available, papers published by the Soil Erosion Laboratory at the University of Moscow indicate a severe and worsening erosion situation.[30]

"Mounting population is pushing
farmers onto lands too steep
to sustain cultivation and too dry to
protect them from winds."

In early 1982, Mikhail Gorbachev, then only a Politburo member, urged planners to heed the advice of soil scientists and adopt measures to limit erosion. But in the face of pressures to reduce food imports— then the world's largest—the scientists often were ignored and responsible management practices cast aside.[31]

19

Soil erosion is making future production gains more difficult in China as well. The Yellow River Conservancy Commission reported in 1983 that the Huang He, or Yellow River, was depositing 1.2 billion tons of soil in the ocean each year. At the Mauna Loa observatory in Hawaii, scientists taking air samples can tell when spring plowing starts in China by the surge of dust carried eastward by prevailing winds.[32]

Perhaps the grimmest soil erosion report came in a 1978 despatch from the U.S. embassy in Addis Ababa stating that an estimated 1 billion tons of topsoil were washing down from Ethiopia's highlands each year. The result for that country has become well known: recurrent famine, a window on the future of other Third World countries that are failing to control soil loss.[33]

The use of land for building is also shrinking the cropland area. In China, one result of the past decade's welcome prosperity is that literally millions of villagers are either expanding their existing dwellings or building new ones. And an industrial sector expanding at more than 12 percent annually since 1980 means the construction of thousands of new factories. Since most of China's 1.1 billion people are concentrated in its rich farming regions, new homes and factories are often built on cropland. This loss of agricultural land combined with the shifts to more profitable crops has reduced the grain growing area 9 percent since 1976.[34]

Throughout the Third World, mounting population pressures are pushing farmers onto lands too steeply sloping to sustain cultivation and semi-arid lands too dry to protect them from the winds when plowed. As erosion continues, land gradually loses its inherent productivity, threatening the livelihood of those who depend on it.[35]

During the eighties, the results of this process have come to be well understood. Researchers now realize that continual overuse of biological systems can set in motion changes that become self-reinforcing. World Bank ecologist Kenneth Newcombe has described how complex systems unravel through several stages, each of which hastens the onset of the next. His model, drawn from the experience of Ethiopia, shows how a decline in biological productivity can be triggered by a loss of tree cover.[36]

All too often, this starts when the firewood demands of growing populations begin to exceed the sustainable yield of local forests. As the woodlands recede from the towns, firewood becomes scarce. At this point, villagers start using crop residues and animal dung for cooking. This interrupts two important cycles, depriving the land of nutrients and also of the organic matter essential to maintaining a productive soil structure. As protective vegetation disappears and as soils become more compact, more rainfall runs off, soil erosion accelerates, less water is absorbed by the soil, and the soil moisture needed for healthy crops diminishes. Water tables begin to fall. Over time, wells go dry. Eventually, there is not enough soil left to support even subsistence-level agriculture. At this point, villagers become environmental refugees, migrating to the nearest city or relief camp.[37]

Official recognition of this cycle of land degradation and its consequences is emerging in India. A study commissioned by its Society for Promotion of Wastelands Development found that 39 percent of that nation's land is now degraded. (See Table 3.) In a 1985 radio address, Prime Minister Rajiv Gandhi reflected the plight of many Third World countries: "Continuing deforestation has brought us face to face with a major ecological and economic crisis. The trend must be halted."[38]

Agronomists in India estimated that their country, with the same cropland area as the United States, was losing some 5 billion tons of topsoil each year as of 1975, compared with a U.S. loss of just over 3 billion tons. Gandhi went on to commission a National Wastelands Development Board charged with turning 5 million hectares of degraded land every year into fuelwood and fodder plantations.[39]

Table 3: Extent of Land Degradation in India, circa 1980

Land Type	Area
	(million hectares)
Degraded nonforested land	94
Saline and alkaline land	7
Wind-eroded land	13
Water-eroded land	74
Degraded forested land	35
Total degraded land	129
National land area	329

Source: D.R. Bhumba and Arvind Khare, *Estimate of Wastelands in India*, Society for Promotion of Wastelands Development, New Delhi, undated.

This grim process of eroding soils is leading the world into a period of agricultural retrenchment. Even ignoring the cropland idled under U.S. commodity programs, the world area in grain has declined steadily since reaching a historical high in 1981. As noted earlier, the United States is in the midst of a five-year program to convert at least 40 million acres (16 million hectares) of highly erodible cropland—11 percent of its total cropland—to grassland or woodland before it loses its topsoil and becomes waste.[40] (See Table 4.)

In contrast to the United States, the Soviet Union does not have a program for converting highly erodible land to less-intensive, but sustainable uses. As a consequence, each year since 1977, it has abandoned roughly a million hectares of cropland, leading to a 13-percent shrinkage in grain area. Abandonment on this scale suggests that a far larger area is likely to be suffering a decline in inherent fertility, helping explain why the Soviets now lead the world in fertilizer use.[41]

Table 4: Sign-up for the Conservation Reserve Program

Sign-up Period	Area Signed Up	Average Annual Rental Rate Per Hectare
	(million hectares)	(dollars)
March 1986	0.30	104
May 1986	1.12	109
August 1986	1.90	116
February 1987	3.84	126
July 1987	2.14	119
February 1988	1.38	119
TOTAL	10.68	119

Sources: U.S. Department of Agriculture, Economic Research Service, *Agricultural Resources: Cropland, Water, and Conservation Situation and Outlook Report* (Washington, D.C.: September 1987); "Sixth CRP Signup Adds 3.4 Million Acres," *Agricultural Outlook*, 1988.

In some Third World countries, cropland degradation from erosion is leading to the wholesale abandonment not only of cropland, but entire villages. Across the southern fringe of the Sahara Desert, thousands of villages and their surrounding farmlands are being surrendered to the sand. As a result of declining rainfall, land degradation, and desertification, the agricultural frontier is retreating southward across a broad band of Africa, stretching from Mauritania in the west to Sudan in the east.[42]

As the eighties draw to a close, such data as are available indicate that soil erosion is slowly reducing the inherent productivity of up to one-third of the world's cropland, though increased use of chemical fertilizers is temporarily masking this deterioration. Worldwide, we estimated in 1984 that farmers were losing 24 billion tons of topsoil from their cropland each year, roughly the amount of topsoil covering Australia's wheat lands.[43]

Water for Irrigation

During the several millennia since irrigation began in the Middle East, it has spread throughout the world. In 1900, some 40 million hectares were irrigated. By 1950, the total had reached 94 million hectares. Over the next three decades, the growth was explosive. Irrigation increased some 2.6 times to 249 million hectares. (See Figure 4.) Since 1980, however, growth has slowed dramatically, expanding by an estimated 8 million hectares.

The 155 million hectares added to the world's irrigated area from 1950 to 1980 entailed the heavy use of both river and underground water resources. Since both of these methods involve large capital commitments, irrigation was a major focus of investment by national governments as well as of lending by international development agencies. In addition, farmers drilling wells on their own land with their own capital in the southern and central Great Plains of the United States and the Gangetic Plain of India contributed to these impressive gains.[44]

The conditions conducive to irrigation from rivers are concentrated in Asia, which has some of the world's great rivers—the Indus, the Ganges, the Brahmaputra, the Chang Jiang (Yangtze), and the Huang He (Yellow). These rivers originate at high elevations and traverse long distances, providing numerous opportunities for dams, and the diversion of water onto the land in a network of gravity-fed canals and ditches, as they flow to the sea. As a result, some two-thirds of the world's irrigated area is in Asia.

China and India lead the world in irrigated land. Irrigated area in China grew impressively between 1950 and 1980, increasing from scarcely 20 million hectares in 1950 to some 48 million by 1980. This growth facilitated an increase in multiple cropping, from an average of 1.3 crops per hectare in 1950 to 1.5 in 1980.[45]

India's net irrigated area in 1950 was 21 million hectares, almost exactly the same as China's. Though growth has been less rapid, its irrigated area nonetheless totalled some 39 million hectares as of 1980. The most

Million
Hectares

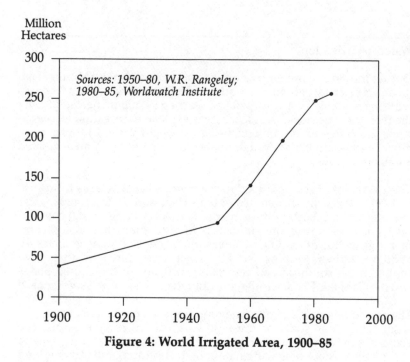

Figure 4: World Irrigated Area, 1900–85

rapid growth has occurred since the mid-sixties, following the intro-
duction of high-yielding wheat and rice varieties that were both more
responsive to the use of water and more exacting in their demands.
This enhanced profitability stimulated widespread investments by
small farmers in wells of their own so they could more fully exploit the
yield potential of the new varieties.[46]

The United States and the Soviet Union rank third and fourth,
respectively, in irrigated area. Growth in the U.S. irrigated area during
the period from 1950 to 1980 was concentrated in the southern Great

Plains, largely based on water from the Ogallala Aquifer, a vast, largely non-replenishable underground water reserve.[47]

25

Soviet irrigated area grew steadily during the same period. With some 18 million hectares already under irrigation in 1983, the Soviet Union planned the addition of over 600,000 hectares a year during the mid-eighties. The Soviets look to irrigation not only to help boost food production but also to minimize the wide swings in crop output that result from highly variable rainfall.[48]

Irrigation often holds the key to cropping intensity, especially in monsoonal climates, where the wet season is followed by several months with little or no rain. Where temperatures permit year-round cropping, as they often do where monsoons prevail, irrigation allows the production of two, three, or even more crops per year.

Unfortunately, not all of the irrigation expansion during the preceding three decades is sustainable. Some, as in the southern Great Plains, is based on the use of fossil water, which will eventually be depleted. In other parts of the United States and in other countries, some irrigation growth has resulted in the drawing down of water tables as pumping exceeds aquifer recharge. In addition, the water available for irrigation is being reduced in still other areas by the growing water demands of industries and cities.[49]

In recent years, the world's two leading food producers—the United States and China—have experienced unplanned declines in irrigated area. The U.S. irrigated area, which peaked in 1978, has fallen some 7 percent since then, reversing several decades of growth. In addition to falling water tables, depressed commodity prices and rising pumping costs have also contributed to the shrinkage. (See Figure 5.) In China, whose irrigated area also peaked in 1978, it has shrunk by some 11 percent, largely due to falling water tables and growing competition from nonfarm uses. There is also evidence of deterioration in some community irrigation systems due to neglect arising from the shift to family-centered farming.[50]

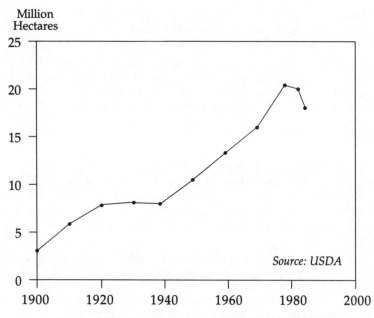

Figure 5: U.S. Irrigated Farmland Area, 1900–84

Further declines in U.S. irrigated area are in prospect. In 1986, the USDA reported that more than one-fourth of the 21 million hectares of irrigated cropland was being watered by pulling down water tables, with the drop ranging from 6 inches to 4 feet per year. They were falling either because the pumping exceeded the rate of aquifer recharge or because the water was from the largely nonrenewable Ogallala Aquifer. Although water mining is an option in the short run, in the long run withdrawals cannot exceed aquifer recharge.[51]

In China, irrigation is threatened by a growing scarcity of fresh water throughout much of the country's northern regions. Under parts of the

North China Plain in the region surrounding Beijing and Tianjin, the water table is dropping by one to two meters per year. Industrial, residential, and agricultural users compete for dwindling supplies of fresh water.[52]

There is also evidence of overpumping in India. Although no groundwater study comparable to the USDA survey has been done, several states have reported that water tables are falling and that wells are going dry. In Tamil Nadu, a water-short state on India's eastern coast, the water table in some areas fell 25–30 meters during the seventies. In Maharashtra, on the west coast, competition is growing between large-scale producers of commercial crops, such as sugar cane, and local villagers who are producing food staples for their own consumption. As commercial growers invest in deeper wells, they lower the water table, and the shallow, hand-dug wells of the villagers go dry. Thousands of Indian villages now rely on tank trucks for their drinking water. Widespread water shortages in some states notwithstanding, there is still a large potential for irrigation expansion in parts of India, such as in the water-rich Gangetic Plain.[53]

In the Soviet Union, the excessive use of water for irrigation takes the form of diminished river flows rather than falling water tables. Most of the nation's irrigated cropland is in central Asia, much of it watered by the Syr-Darya and Amu-Darya, the two great rivers of the region. Irrigation diversions from these rivers have greatly reduced their flow into the land-locked Aral Sea. As a result, the sea's water level has fallen some 12 meters since heavy river diversions got underway some two decades ago.[54]

The Aral has shrunk to half its original size. Muniak, once a port city and major fish-processing center, is now nearly 50 kilometers from the shoreline. Soviet scientists fear a major ecological catastrophe is unfolding as the sea slowly disappears. The dry bottom is now becoming desert, the site of sand storms that may drop up to half a ton per hectare of a sand-salt mix on the surrounding fields—damaging the very crops that water once destined for the sea is used to grow.[55]

The Soviet Union's prospects for future irrigation expansion are limited. Two years ago, the government abandoned its ambitious plan to divert southward into Central Asia the Siberian rivers that flow into the Arctic Ocean. Although investment in irrigation continues, the prospective net gains are modest ones.[56]

Apart from the growing scarcity of fresh water, the productivity of perhaps one-third of the world's irrigated land is being adversely affected by severe waterlogging and salting. Like soil erosion, this process at first gradually reduces land productivity and eventually leads to abandonment.[57]

If underground drainage of irrigated land is not adequate, percolation from river water diverted onto farmland gradually accumulates and over time slowly raises the water table until it moves to within a few feet of the surface. As a result, deep-rooted crops begin to suffer. As the water table continues to rise, it begins evaporating through the remaining inches of soil into the atmosphere, leaving salt on the surface and reducing the land's productivity.

With all natural water containing a certain amount of salt, the buildup of salt is a common threat to the sustainability of irrigated agriculture. As long as the hydrodynamics of the irrigation system provide sufficient flushing, salt does not accumulate in the surface soil. But in many semi-arid and arid regions, this is not the case. Glistening white expanses of salt-covered cropland, once highly productive but now abandoned, can be seen when flying over Pakistan and the Middle East.[58]

Worldwide, the prospects for major gains in irrigated area are not good. Irrigated area in the world's two major food producers, the United States and China, has declined in recent years and may well drop further.[59]

India's irrigated area is projected to expand steadily in the years ahead. The Soviet Union's continuing investment in irrigation will lead to some modest increases. And in several of the smaller countries of Asia, such as Thailand and the Philippines, naturally flooded riceland is being converted to irrigated riceland, a shift that permits farmers to raise yields dramatically. At least some developing countries on each continent are planning new additions to their irrigated land. As food prices rise, investment in irrigation will also rise.

On balance, however, it now seems unlikely that the world will be able to reestablish a trend of rapid, sustained gains in irrigated area of the sort that characterized the period from 1950 to 1980. In retrospect, this three-decade growth era will likely be seen as unique.

Depletion of fossil aquifers, falling water tables, growing competition for water from nonfarm sources, and the abandonment of severely salted irrigated land suggest that only modest increases in irrigation lie ahead. To the extent that the irrigated area does expand, it may depend as much on gains in water-use efficiency as on new supplies.

The Land Productivity Potential

The ancients calculated yield as the ratio of grain harvested to that sown. For them, the scarce resource was the seed grain itself. In the late twentieth century, land is becoming the constraint. The key to satisfying future needs is raising land productivity.

With little opportunity to add productive land to the world's cultivated area, the food prospect in the nineties is directly tied to the potential for raising land productivity. Between 1950 and 1984, farmers more than doubled the productivity of their cropland. World grain yield per hectare increased from 1.1 metric tons to 2.3 metric tons, a remarkable feat. (See Figure 6.)

Since 1984, however, there has been little change in grain yields. One reason is undoubtedly the depressed level of farm prices during this period, which has discouraged both short-term investment in inputs, such as fertilizer, and longer-term investments in land improvement. And the monsoon failure in India in 1987 and the droughts in North America and China in 1988 depressed the global average yield.

Kilograms

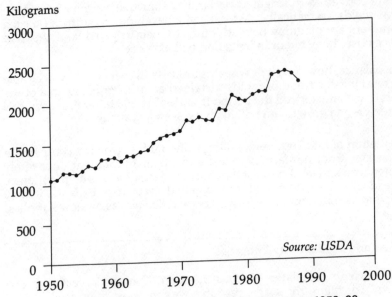

Figure 6. World Grain Yield Per Hectare, 1950–88

However, as grain prices rise, as they are already doing in 1988, grain yields should resume their long-term rise.[60]

By far the most important source of rising grain yields in recent decades has been the growth in fertilizer use. From 1950 through 1984, world fertilizer use moved higher each year, with only occasional interruption. Since then, though, the pattern has become somewhat erratic, as agricultural commodity prices weakened, Third World debt soared, the yield response to fertilizer use diminished, and many financially pressed governments reduced fertilizer subsidies.[61]

World fertilizer use increased from 14 million tons to 125 million tons between 1950 and 1984, a ninefold gain, or more than 11 percent per year. Between 1984 and 1988, it increased from 125 million tons to 135 million tons, a gain of less than 2 percent per year. (See Table 5.)

In per capita terms, world fertilizer use quintupled between 1950 and 1984, going from 5 kilograms to 26 kilograms, offsetting a one-third decline in grain area per person. As land becomes scarce, farmers rely more on the use of additional fertilizer to expand output, in effect substituting energy in the form of fertilizer for land in the production process. (See Figure 7.)

During the fifties and most of the sixties, growth in world fertilizer use was concentrated in the industrial world. As the adoption of high-yielding, fertilizer-responsive varieties of wheat and rice gained momentum in Asia, so too, did fertilizer use. In some agriculturally advanced countries, fertilizer use has actually declined in recent years. In the United States, for example, fertilizer use peaked in 1981 and has fallen since then as farm prices have weakened.[62]

In China, now the world's second largest food producer, meaningful expansion in the use of chemical fertilizer did not begin until 1960, when planners realized that even the most assiduous use of organic fertilizer could not produce enough food to sustain the country's growing population. As new fertilizer plants came on line in the late seventies, usage climbed sharply, more than doubling between 1976 and 1981—the steepest increase ever in a major food-producing country.[63]

Nevertheless, organic fertilizer continues to be a major source of plant nutrients in China. Over half of the country's organic fertilizer comes from livestock manure, principally that of pigs and draft animals. Human waste, green manure crops—those grown only to raise soil fertility—and compost make up most of the remainder.[64]

In contrast to water and land, there are no immediately foreseeable constraints on the use of major chemical nutrients—nitrogen, phosphate, or potash—except for those imposed by the availability and cost of the energy needed to manufacture these fertilizers.

Table 5: World Fertilizer Use, Total and Per Capita, 1950–86

Year	Total	Per Capita
	(million metric tons)	(kilograms)
1950	14	5
1955	18	7
1960	27	9
1965	40	12
1970	63	17
1975	82	21
1980	112	26
1981	116	26
1982	115	25
1983	115	24
1984	125	26
1985	130	26
1986	129	26
1987	131	26
1988	135	26

Sources: U.N. Food and Agriculture Organization, *FAO Fertilizer Yearbook* (Rome: various years); FAO, *Current World Fertilizer Situation and Outlook 1985/86–1991/92* (Rome: 1987).

With little prospect of any substantial additions to the world's cropland over the remainder of this century, the question of how much land productivity can be raised is the key to the world food prospect. Some sense of the potential can be gleaned from looking at yield trends for wheat, rice, and corn in countries with the highest yield levels—for

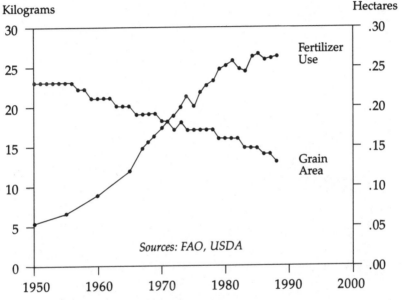

**Figure 7: World Fertilizer Use and Grain Area
Per Capita, 1950–88**

example, rice in Japan, corn in the United States, and wheat in the United Kingdom. (See Figure 8.)

In 1950, crop yields in these countries were essentially the same, at about 2.25 metric tons per hectare. Over time, the Japanese rice yield increased slowly, reaching 4 tons per hectare in the mid-seventies. Since then, it has increased relatively little, even though the government support price is far above the world market price.

A similar trend exists in other high-technology rice producing countries, such as South Korea, Taiwan, and Italy. In each case, once rice yields pass 4 tons per hectare, they rise quite slowly or even level off, suggesting that dramatically raising rice yields above this level may

Kilograms

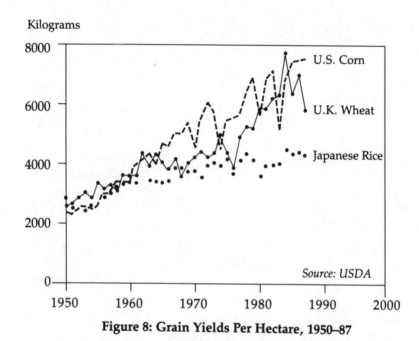

Figure 8: Grain Yields Per Hectare, 1950–87

await new technological advances. Agricultural economists Duane Chapman and Randy Barker of Cornell point out that "the genetic yield potential of rice has not increased significantly since the release of the high yielding varieties in 1966."[65]

With both corn and wheat, yields have gone much higher. Corn yields in the United States, for example, have exceeded 7 tons per hectare in good crop years. Likewise, wheat in the United Kingdom has ranged between 6 and 7 or more tons per hectare in recent years, rising above 7 tons only once.[66]

At this point, no one knows how far yields can profitably be raised. Eventually, growth in yield per hectare, like the growth of any other

"The question of how much land
productivity can be raised is the key
to the world food prospect."

biological process in a finite environment, will conform to the S-shaped
curve. What is not clear is how close yields in the higher-yield
countries are to the upper inflection point on this curve.

35

The systematic application of science to agriculture and the increasing
investment of energy in agricultural inputs and processes has permitted a regular yearly increase in yields for more than a generation,
making it difficult to imagine a situation where yields will not continue
their steady rise. Nonetheless, some analysts are becoming concerned
about the potential for indefinitely raising yields, a concern heightened
by the limited potential for finding new cropland.[67]

Robert Herdt, senior economist at the Rockefeller Foundation, antici-
pates a slowdown in grain production growth in the developing
countries. He observes that "in the next five to ten years there is little
potential for further rapid spread of existing semi-dwarf varieties that
provided the breakthrough in developing-country wheat and rice
production in the mid-1960s. Likewise, it appears that there is little
scope for increasing the rates of fertilizer [application] on those
varieties much above their mid-1980s levels."[68]

In some farming communities crop yields on the best farms now
approach those on experimental plots. It is unrealistic, however, to
expect yields on farms actually to reach those of experimental plots.
The latter are used to determine the maximum physical response to
an input, such as fertilizer. Farmers, on the other hand, are concerned
with the maximum profit response. Scientists working on experimental plots can increase fertilizer use until there is no more response.
Farmers cannot increase fertilizer use beyond the point where the
profit from the additional yield does not cover the cost of the additional
fertilizer.

Similarly, scientists on experimental plots can plant during the period
that will produce maximum yields. Farmers, who must deal with
real-world constraints, such as multiple-cropping and the demands
on their time imposed by other crops, often cannot plant during this
narrow window.

Rising grain yield per hectare, like any other biological process, must eventually give way to physical constraints. With cereal yields, the ultimate limit may be photosynthetic efficiency. Where the best farmers supply all the nutrients and water that advanced varieties can use, cereal yields may now be approaching this limit.

Evidence that photosynthetic constraints may be emerging can be seen in the diminishing returns on fertilizer use. Whereas 20 years ago the application of each additional ton of fertilizer in the U.S. corn belt added 15 to 20 tons to the world grain harvest, today it may add only 6 to 10 tons. In analyzing recent agricultural trends in Indonesia, Chapman and Barker note that "while one kilogram of fertilizer nutrients probably led to a yield increase of 10 kilograms of unmilled rice in 1972, this ratio has fallen to about one to five at present." This, combined with depressed farm prices, helps explain why growth in world fertilizer use has slowed in recent years and why it has actually declined in some countries, including the United States.[69]

Hybrid wheats and rices have been available for many years but, except for hybrid rice in China, their widespread use awaits far higher grain prices. And since yields of the more productive wheat and rice strains now in use are much closer to the photosynthetic limit than were those of corn when hybrids were introduced 50 years ago, the potential for raising output is comparatively modest.

Other possibilities for boosting output lie in breeding cereals more tolerant of salt or drought. Gains from this source will raise output only where plants are subject to these stresses, but in a food-short world every small gain will help.

Contrary to popular opinion, biotechnology is not an agricultural panacea that will end hunger. For instance, the development of nitrogen-fixing cereals, which biotechnological techniques could facilitate, would reduce the need for fertilizer but would also likely lower yields, since some of the plant's metabolic energy is diverted to fixing nitrogen rather than producing seed. Biotechnology is a timely addition to the scientist's tool kit, one that will speed the pace and the potential return on investment in agricultural research, but it does not

"Other possibilities for boosting output
lie in breeding cereals
more tolerant of salt or drought."

promise dramatic production gains. The contribution of this research tool, like all the others that scientists use, is ultimately constrained by the limits of photosynthetic efficiency.

Unfortunately, there are no identifiable technologies waiting in the wings that will lead to the quantum jumps in world food output such as those associated with the spread of hybrid corn, the ninefold increase in fertilizer use between 1950 and 1984, the near tripling of irrigated area during the same period, or the relatively recent spread of the high-yielding dwarf wheats and rices in Third World countries. The contribution of these technologies is playing out in some situations and there are no major new technologies emerging to take their place.

Although countries where yields are already quite high are finding it difficult to maintain a rapid rise, those where yields are low can tap existing technologies to boost their output. For example, Japan may not be much more successful in raising rice yields in the nineties than it has been in the late eighties, but India, where rice yields are less than half those of Japan, still has a large unrealized potential.[70]

Food and Climate Change

Farmers, who have always had to deal with the vagaries of weather, now also face the unsettling prospect of climate change. Agriculture has evolved over a 10,000-year period of remarkable climate stability. Any major departure from those conditions will cause enormous hardship and require incalculable investments during the adjustment.

There are two climate-related questions now facing world agriculture. First, is the long-projected warming, as a result of the buildup in greenhouse gases, now underway? And, second, how will the warming affect agriculture?

The first question was addressed in late June 1988 by one of the country's leading climate modelers, James Hansen, head of NASA's Goddard Institute of Space Studies. In testimony before the U.S. Senate Committee on Energy and Natural Resources, Hansen said that he is 99 percent certain that we are now seeing the greenhouse effect. He pointed out that the four warmest years of the past century have occurred during the eighties. And data for the first half of 1988 indicate that it is likely to be the warmest on record. Hansen also noted that these observed higher temperatures are what the models project for current levels of greenhouse gases.[71]

When queried in August 1988 on Hansen's statement about the certainty of the greenhouse effect, John Firor, director of advanced studies at the National Center for Atmospheric Research in Boulder, Colorado, said that "one reason Hansen could make that statement was the spectacular convergence of scientific opinion." He went on to say that "there is just no disagreement that we're in for a rapid heating. The only question is how much."[72] Although not all scientists agree with Hansen and Firor, the weight of scientific opinion is clearly shifting in their direction.

For the second question, we turn to the general circulation models of the earth's atmosphere that are used to simulate the effects on climate of various developments, including the buildup of greenhouse gases. The most advanced global-climate models indicate that a doubling of the pre-industrial level of carbon dioxide, or the equivalent when the effect of other greenhouse gases is taken into account, would raise the global temperature by between 1.5 and 4.5 degrees Celsius (2.7 to 8.1 degrees Fahrenheit). If the world continues on a business-as-usual path, the most recent projections show this occurring as early as 2030, a point closer in time than the end of World War II.[73]

These temperature rises are global averages, but scientists now agree that the increase in temperature would not be spread evenly, but would be far greater in the middle and higher latitudes and greater over the land than over the ocean. Temperatures near the equator are projected to change very little as the earth warms, while rises in the higher latitudes could easily be twice the average projected for the globe as a whole. Most of the world's food is produced in the northern hemisphere, and most of it within the middle and higher latitudes. Relatively little is produced near the equator, where climate change would be least.[74]

> "Most of the world's food is produced in the middle and higher latitudes of the northern hemisphere, where the warming could be greatest."

According to Hansen, the observed increase in mid-continental summer dryness during the eighties is consistent with climate changes predicted by the models as a result of the rising level of greenhouse gasses in the atmosphere.[75]

Though they remain sketchy, meteorological models suggest that two of the world's major food-producing regions—the North American agricultural heartland and the principal grain-growing regions of the Soviet Union—are likely to experience a decline in soil moisture during the summer growing season as a result of reduced rainfall and higher temperatures. In addition to their contribution to evaporation, higher than usual temperatures can impair cereal pollination and thus reduce yields. In an article scheduled to appear in the *Journal of Geophysical Research*, Hansen and his colleagues say their model shows that the land areas where an unambiguous warming appears earliest as the greenhouse gas buildup proceeds are China and parts of Central Asia. The record-high, crop-damaging temperatures experienced during the summer of 1988 in central China are consistent with this modeling result.[76]

If the warming unfolds as the models indicate it will, much of the land in the western U.S. Great Plains that now produces wheat would revert to grassland. The western U.S. corn belt would become semiarid, with wheat or other drought-tolerant grains that yield 2.5 metric tons per hectare replacing corn, which yields 6 or more tons. Land values would drop in anticipation of the shift to less-productive crops. On the plus side, as temperatures increase the winter wheat belt would shift northward, with winter wheat yielding 2.7 tons per hectare replacing spring wheat yielding just under 2.0 tons per hectare. A longer growing season would also permit a northward extension of spring wheat production in areas such as Canada's Alberta Province, thus increasing the cultivated area.

One of the highest costs facing world agriculture would be the adjustment of irrigation and drainage systems. As the warming proceeds and rainfall patterns change, both these systems would become redundant in some situations and inadequate in others. According to an analysis by my colleague Sandra Postel in *State of the*

World 1987, adjusting irrigation systems alone might require an investment of some $200 billion worldwide.[77]

40   The most immediate result of the warming of the earth would be the effect of higher temperatures on evaporation rates and crop growth. Over the longer term, however, as the oceans slowly absorb heat from the atmosphere, they too would begin to warm. Along with the melting of glaciers and parts of polar ice caps, the ensuing thermal expansion will raise the sea level. This would endanger that share of the Asian rice harvest that is produced on low-lying river floodplains and deltas. The loss of cropland through flooding or saltwater incursion will only make it more difficult to feed the region's 2.9 billion people.

Whether the drought conditions of 1988 are likely to be repeated soon is of interest not only to farmers of the United States and Canada, but to consumers throughout the world, given their dependence on grain from North America. Drought is defined as dryness, a condition that can result from lower than normal rainfall, higher than normal temperatures, or both. Even with normal rainfall in the U.S. Midwest and Great Plains in 1988, moderate drought conditions would have prevailed during the summer because of unusually high temperatures. Day after day of record-high temperatures from the Atlantic Coast to the Rocky Mountains during the summer of 1988 would have reduced harvests in any event. When above-normal temperatures are combined with below-normal rainfall, as they were in 1988, yield reductions can be severe.[78]

An examination of U.S. yields since 1950 of corn, which accounts for two-thirds of U.S. grain production and one-eighth of that for the world, shows five harvests down sharply from the preceding year. (See Figure 9.) The only two pronounced drops in corn yields before the eighties came in 1970, a result of a corn blight, and in 1974, when a wet spring and late planting combined with an early frost to destroy a part of the crop before it matured.

Three harvests have been severely reduced by drought, all in the eighties, each progressively more severe. Compared with the preced-

Kilograms

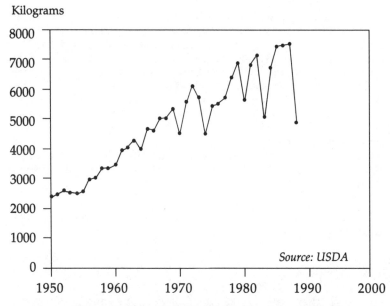

Figure 9: U.S. Corn Yield Per Hectare, 1950–88

ing year, the 1980 corn yield per hectare was down by 17 percent, that in 1983 was down by 28 percent, and that in 1988 by a staggering 35 percent. Each of these three drought-reduced harvests occurred during one of the five years—1980, 1981, 1983, 1987, and 1988—that are described as the warmest for the world during the last century. Although it is tempting to assume that this is not a coincidence, there is no scientific way of linking the warming and the drought-depressed U.S. harvests, since annual weather variability is so much greater than the modest rise in average global temperatures measured during the eighties.[79]

However, if the warming is indeed underway, as many meteorologists now believe, then drought-reduced harvests of the sort experienced three times during the eighties could become more frequent.[80]

Among other things, the prospect of climate change increases uncertainty over harvest prospects for farmers and policymakers alike. For example, the 1989 U.S. grain crop could be a bin-busting one, the largest ever received. With a normal harvest elsewhere in the world, this would permit at least a modest rebuilding of depleted grain reserves. Or it could be even smaller than the drought-reduced harvest of 1988. If a warming is underway and 1989 is warmer than 1988, just as it in turn was warmer than 1987, drought and heat could be even more destructive. If 1989 follows in the trend of the three drought-reduced harvests during the eighties, each more severe than the preceding one, the world would be in some difficulty, faced with the need for emergency measures to cut back grain use among the affluent to ensure that the poor do not starve.

Food Security Trends

The two most useful global indicators of food security are per capita grain production and carryover stocks of grain—the amount in the bin when the new harvest begins. The trend in per capita production gives a sense of whether overall food availability is improving or deteriorating. Changes in carryover stocks indicate whether production is exceeding consumption or the opposite.

World grain production per person climbed steadily between the early sixties and the late seventies. Since 1978, however, it has increased little. It reached an all-time high in 1984 of 345 kilograms, then declined slightly in 1985 and 1986 before dropping sharply in 1987 and again in 1988. The decline in total grain production in 1988—largely the result of the droughts in North America and China—completed the largest two-year drop on record. The accompanying 14-percent fall in per capita production since 1984 brought this indicator back to the levels of the mid-seventies. (See Figure 10.)

This look at global changes in per capita production, however, obscures wide differences in regional trends. For example, as noted earlier, while per capita production in Western Europe was climbing

Kilograms

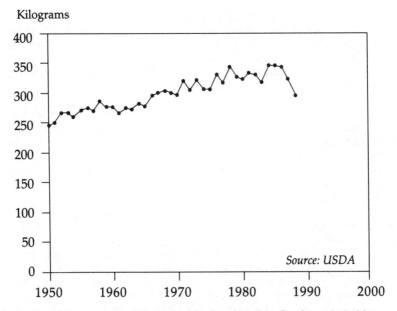

Figure 10: World Grain Production Per Capita, 1950–88

rapidly, that in Africa peaked in 1967 and has declined some 27 percent since then. These two regions illustrate the extremes.[81]

Unfortunately, Latin America has joined Africa during the eighties as the second region to experience a continual decline in food production per person. Latin America's peak came in 1981, the year before the debt crisis began. Since then it has fallen some 13 percent, expanding the region's grain deficit.[82]

As total grain production has declined during the last two years, so too have stocks. World carryover stocks reached an all-time high in 1987 of 459 million tons, enough to feed the world for 101 days. During 1987, stocks dropped to 390 million tons. In 1988, we estimate that world consumption will exceed production by a staggering 152 million tons. (See Table 6.) Unless the mid-year USDA world grain consumption estimate of 1,672 million tons is reduced by rising prices, year-end stocks are expected to fall to roughly 250 million tons. This amounts to 54 days of consumption, less than the 57-day supply at the end of 1972 when world grain prices doubled.

At 54 days of consumption, carryover stocks amount to little more than "pipeline" supplies. Substantial quantities of grain are required to keep the supply line between producer and consumer filled, lest supplies be interrupted. The supply lines from the United States, which holds a disproportionately large share of the world's carryover stocks in order to assure regular supplies to its customers, often stretch halfway around the world.

In addition to its carryover stocks, the world has a second line of defense against food shortages—the cropland idled under U.S. commodity programs. In 1988 some 20 million hectares (50 million acres) were idled under farm programs designed to maintain price stability. (See Table 7.) Virtually all of this land can be returned to production within one year if the USDA decides it is needed. Amounting to roughly 2 percent of the world cropland area, this reserve can help boost production now that stocks are depleted. Given the precariously low level of carryover stocks, prudence argues for returning this land to production in 1989. The 10 million hectares of highly erodible cropland that has been planted to grass or trees since early 1986 under the Conservation Reserve Program should not be disturbed.[83]

As stocks have dropped, higher prices and scarce supplies increasingly pose a serious threat to those food-importing countries with low incomes. When carryover stocks hit 57 days at the end of 1972, the United States returned its idled cropland to use. Four years passed, however, before world grain reserves were rebuilt and food-importing countries could again breathe easily.

Thus, the devastated grain crop in North America in 1988 is sobering news for the more than 100 countries that depend on imports from the North American breadbasket. For the poorer food-deficit countries,

Table 6: World Grain Production, Use and Carryover Stocks, 1961–88

Year	Production	Consump-tion	Carryover Stocks	Days of Consump-tion
		(million metric tons)		(days)
1961	813	835	185	81
1965	917	952	159	61
1970	1,096	1,130	198	64
1971	1,194	1,169	223	70
1972	1,155	1,192	186	57
1973	1,271	1,259	198	57
1974	1,219	1,213	203	61
1975	1,250	1,229	221	66
1976	1,363	1,303	281	79
1977	1,337	1,338	279	76
1978	1,467	1,418	328	84
1979	1,428	1,440	315	80
1980	1,447	1,475	286	71
1981	1,497	1,476	307	76
1982	1,548	1,500	355	86
1983	1,485	1,537	303	72
1984	1,645	1,585	363	84
1985	1,661	1,594	430	98
1986	1,682	1,653	459	101
1987	1,597	1,653	402	89
1988	1,521	1,673	250	54

45

Sources: 1961–87, U.S. Department of Agriculture, Foreign Agricultural Service, *World Grain Situation and Outlook* (Washington, D.C.: July 1988); 1988, Worldwatch Institute.

Table 7: Cropland Idled Under U.S. Commodity Programs, 1965–88

Year	Land Area
	(hectares)
1965	17.4
1966	19.3
1967	10.2
1968	14.5
1969	20.3
1970	21.5
1971	13.7
1972	23.8
1973	6.8
1974	0.0
1975	0.0
1976	0.0
1977	0.0
1978	7.4
1979	5.3
1980	0.0
1981	0.0
1982	4.5
1983	31.5
1984	10.9
1985	12.5
1986	17.5
1987	21.7
1988	20.1

Source: Brad Karmen, U.S. Department of Agriculture, private communication, June 24, 1988.

"In the drought-stricken year of 1988,
the U.S. grain harvest has fallen below
domestic consumption—probably for
the first time in history."

many with external debts that are already unmanageable, maintaining needed imports in the face of dramatic price rises may not be possible. For people living in these countries, the road to the next harvest could be a long one.

47

Aside from the depletion of world grain stocks, the overwhelming dependence on North America, where agricultural output in both the United States and Canada is affected by the same climatic cycle, introduces a special dimension of food insecurity. A drought in the United States is invariably accompanied by one in Canada. In 1988, when the U.S. grain harvest was down 31 percent, that of Canada was down by 27 percent. With the United States and Canada controlling a larger share of grain exports than the Middle East does of oil, this is an issue of concern to food-importing countries everywhere.[84]

The risk in depending heavily on North America is evident in Table 8. During the eighties, North American grain exports have averaged around 110 million tons per year. Even with this level of exports, there has been some U.S. cropland idled during most of the eighties.

In the drought-stricken year of 1988, however, the U.S. grain harvest has fallen below domestic consumption, probably for the first time in history. With a harvest of 190 million tons and an estimated consumption of 202 million tons, there is no surplus for export from the 1988 crop. Export demands until the 1989 harvest begins are being met almost entirely by drawing down stocks. Without reserves to draw upon, this 12-million-ton shortfall would also have forced a reduction in domestic consumption, or the importation of grain if it were available.

The obvious question is, What will happen if there is a severe drought in 1989? Historically, the odds against severe back-to-back droughts have been rather high, but with the warming now apparently underway, the frequency of hot, dry summers is increasing. In the event of even a moderate drought in North America, world food prices would soar. In the event of a severe drought, the world would face a food emergency.

Table 8: United States Grain Production, Consumption and Exportable Surplus by Crop Year, 1984–88

Year	Production	Consumption	Exportable Surplus from Current Crop[1]
	(million metric tons)		
1984	313	197	116
1985	345	201	144
1986	314	216	97
1987	277	211	66
1988	190	202	−12

[1]Does not include carryover stocks.

Sources: U.S. Department of Agriculture, Economic Research Service, *World Grain Harvested Area, Production, and Yield 1950–87* (unpublished printout) (Washington, D.C.: 1988); USDA, Foreign Agricultural Service, *World Grain Situation and Outlook*, August 1988.

In sum, overall global food security is being threatened by two trends. One is the loss of momentum in the growth in food output, a loss that is particularly noticeable in major Third World countries, such as China, India, Indonesia, and Mexico. The second trend is the warming of the planet. The areas that are likely to experience higher temperatures and lower rainfall include some of the world's key food-producing regions, such as mid-continental North America. The world's farmers—already struggling to keep up with the record year-to-year growth in population—are facing the nineties with a great deal of uncertainty about how quickly the warming will progress and how it will affect their food production.

Looking at the Nineties

In many ways, the nineties will be quite unlike any decade that the world's farmers have ever faced. There will be little opportunity for expanding the cultivated area. Irrigated area, the key to higher yields in many countries, is likely to be growing slowly worldwide but actually declining in some key countries. For the world's more advanced farmers, there are not many new technologies to draw upon. On the demand side of the food-population equation, the annual **49** growth in world population is projected to be greater during the early nineties than at any time in history. And, finally, the prospect of a human-induced warming of the earth now hangs over the future of agriculture.[85]

The answer to the question of what can be done to reverse the decline in food security during the last four years begins with the need to protect the cropland base, both from conversion to nonfarm uses and from the erosion that reduces its inherent productivity. Nearly a decade ago, then Assistant Secretary of Agriculture Rupert Cutler observed that "asphalt is the land's last crop."[86] Once productive cropland is lost to nonfarm uses, it is difficult to restore it to food production. A few countries, such as Japan, have carefully crafted programs designed to protect their cropland. In 1968, Japan adopted a comprehensive zoning plan that put all land in one of three categories—industrial, agricultural, and other. Faced with acute pressures on land, Japan confronted the issue early and in doing so established an approach to cropland conservation that is simple, effective, and easily adapted to conditions in other countries.[87]

National success stories in the effort to conserve the topsoil on cropland are few. Among the major food-producing countries, the United States is the only one with a program that is systematically reducing excessive soil erosion. Its Conservation Reserve Program both converts highly erodible cropland to grassland or woodland and penalizes farmers who do not manage their soil responsibly by denying them the benefits from farm programs, including price supports, crop insurance, and low-interest loans. In 1987, the CRP's second year, it helped reduce U.S. soil losses by 460 million tons, the greatest year-to-year reduction in U.S. history.[88]

As fresh water for irrigation becomes more scarce, investment in the increased efficiency of water use will become more attractive. Leakage from irrigation canals and ditches, and the use of inefficient irrigation technologies, present obvious opportunities for investment. There is now a need for research and demonstration projects in raising the productivity of water similar to that used over the past generation to raise the productivity of land. Israel, with its underground drip system and other advanced irrigation technologies, has expanded its irrigated area by using available water supplies more efficiently.[89]

Another measure to increase efficiency in agriculture is nutrient recycling. All too often, the nutrients contained in the food supplies that sustain large cities end up being discharged into local waterways, where they create pollution problems. Many cities in Asia, such as Shanghai and Seoul, systematically recycle human waste onto the farmland immediately surrounding the city. Shanghai now is essentially self-sufficient in vegetables produced in this manner. By reducing the need for chemical fertilizer, comprehensive recycling of nutrients reduces the energy used in agriculture.[90]

At the policy level, there are still many countries whose agricultural price policies do not encourage investment in agriculture. Argentina is perhaps the classic case of a country that taxes agricultural exports, thus discouraging farmers by reducing the prices they receive to levels well below those of the world market. In the Soviet Union, reforms that strengthen the link between effort and reward for those working the land could substantially increase the productivity of agriculture. A plan to lease land to individual farmers for up to 50 years, as announced in Moscow in August 1988, could quickly lift farm output, perhaps even eliminating the need to import grain.[91]

Also high on the list of needed policy revisions for some countries is land reform. World Bank studies in several countries demonstrate that farmers with small holdings produce more per hectare than those with large holdings. In part, this is because small farmers can use much more labor per hectare, thus raising land productivity.[92]

On the research front, perhaps the major contribution of scientists during the nineties will be to help push back the physical frontiers of cropping. This involves the development of varieties that are more drought-resistant, salt-tolerant, and early-maturing. In a warmer world,

"The responsibility for future food
security will shift from farmers to family
planners and energy policymakers."

with sea level rising, the payoff on the first two could be much higher
than in the past.

There is now a need to harness more systematically the potentials of **51**
biotechnology in the effort to ensure future food supplies. At present,
the majority of biotechnology research in agriculture is concentrated
in the hands of agribusiness firms, many of whom are skillfully
exploiting its potential to increase food production. But, unfortunately,
their efforts are concentrated largely in the industrialized countries,
not in rural Africa or Latin America, where food production per person
is falling.

Perhaps the biggest change in the agricultural prospect as the world
enters the nineties is the shift in responsibility for future food security
from farmers to family planners and energy planners. Agricultural
policymakers and farmers acting alone may not be able to ensure
adequate food supplies.

Ministers of energy will have a greater influence on the rate of climate
change and, therefore, perhaps, on future food production trends than
will ministers of agriculture. In the interest of securing future food
supplies, it is now time to move quickly to reduce the use of fossil fuels.

Even with an all-out effort, farmers may not be able to reverse the
falling food production per person that is underway in Africa and Latin
America and that is threatening the Indian subcontinent, unless they
can get help from family planners. What is needed is a major assist of
the sort that China's family planning ministry has provided its farmers
over the last decade, a lift that, when combined with economic reforms
in agriculture, has helped raise food output per person by nearly half
within a decade.[93]

Ensuring adequate food supplies during the nineties and beyond will
require far more of the attention of political leaders, particularly those
in the Third World, than ever before. Unless national governments are
prepared to wage the war against hunger on a far broader front, it may
not be possible to arrest the decline in per capita food production that
is now undermining the future of so many poor countries.

Notes

1. U.S. Department of Agriculture (USDA), Foreign Agricultural Service (FAS), *World Grain Situation and Outlook*, Washington, D.C., August 1988.

2. USDA, Economic Research Service (ERS), *World Grain Harvested Area, Production, and Yield 1950–87* (unpublished printout)(Washington, D.C.: 1988).

3. USDA, FAS, *World Grain Situation and Outlook*, August 1988.

4. USDA, National Agricultural Statistics Service (NASS), *Crop Production*, Washington, D.C., August 1988; James E. Hansen, *The Greenhouse Effect: Impacts on Current Global Temperature and Regional Heat Waves*, statement before the Committee on Energy and Natural Resources, U.S. Senate, June 23, 1988; Syukuro Manabe, *Climate Warming Due to Greenhouse Gases*, statement before the Subcommittee on Toxic Substances and Environmental Oversight, U.S. Senate, December 10, 1985.

5. USDA, ERS, *World Grain*.

6. International Monetary Fund (IMF), *International Financial Statistics*, Washington, D.C., various issues; USDA, FAS, *World Grain Situation and Outlook*, August 1988.

7. USDA, ERS, *An Economic Analysis of USDA Erosion Control Programs* (Washington, D.C., August 1986); Gordon Sloggett and Clifford Dickason, *Ground-Water Mining in the United States* (Washington, D.C.: USDA, ERS, August 1986).

8. Gary A. Margheim, *Implementing Conservation Compliance* (Washington, D.C.: USDA, Soil Conservation Service (SCS), December 1986); "Farmers Turn Down the Irrigation Tap," *Farmline*, August 1988; Sloggett and Dickason, *Ground-Water Mining*.

9. Worldwatch Institute estimate based on irrigation data from Sloggett and Dickason, *Ground-Water Mining*, soil erosion data from USDA, ERS, *An Economic Analysis*, grain production data from USDA, ERS, *World Grain*.

10. Francis Urban and Philip Rose, *World Population by Country and Region, 1950–86, and Projections to 2050* (Washington, D.C.: USDA, ERS, April 1988); USDA, ERS, *World Grain*.

11. Per capita data through 1987 from USDA, ERS, *World Grain*; per capita figure for 1988 derived from USDA, FAS, *World Grain Situation and Outlook*, August 1988, and Urban and Rose, *World Population*.

12. USDA, ERS, *World Grain*.

13. USDA, ERS, *World Grain*; "China Grain Yield Likely to Drop Below Target," *Journal of Commerce*, June 15, 1988; USDA, ERS, *China: Agriculture and Trade Report*, Washington, D.C., June 1988; USDA, ERS, *World Grain*.

14. USDA, ERS, *World Grain*; Bruce Goldstein, "Indonesia Reconsiders Resettlement," *World Watch*, March/April 1988.

15. USDA, ERS, *World Grain*.

16. Ibid.

17. USDA, ERS, *China: Situation and Outlook Report*, Washington, D.C., July 1986.

18. USDA, FAS, *World Grain Situation and Outlook*, August 1986 and January 1987; USDA, FAS, *World Rice Reference Tables* (unpublished printout)(Washington, D.C.: July 1988); USDA, FAS, *World Wheat and Coarse Grains Reference Tables* (unpublished printout)(Washington, D.C.: August 1988).

19. USDA, ERS, *World Grain*; World Bank, *World Development Report 1988* (New York: Oxford University Press, 1988); USDA, ERS, *China: Situation and Outlook Report*, July 1986; USDA, ERS, *China: Agriculture and Trade Report*, June 1988; "Midsummer Heat Brings Problems," *China Daily*, August 4, 1988.

20. USDA, ERS, *China: Situation and Outlook Report*, July 1986; USDA, ERS, *World Grain*.

21. USDA, FAS, *World Rice*; USDA, FAS, *World Wheat and Coarse Grains*.

22. Ibid.

23. Ibid.; United Nations World Food Council (WFC), *The Global State of Hunger and Malnutrition: 1988 Report* (Fourteenth Ministerial Session, Nicosia, Cyprus: March 24, 1988).

24. Population Reference Bureau, *1988 World Population Data Sheet* (Washington, D.C.: 1988); USDA, ERS, *World Grain*.

25. Population Reference Bureau, *1988 World Population Data Sheet*.

26. USDA, ERS, *World Grain*; human caloric intake derived from data in Food and Agriculture Organization of the United Nations (FAO), *FAO Production Yearbook*, 1986; USDA, ERS, *World Grain*; USDA, FAS, *World Grain Situation and Outlook*, August 1988.

27. Calculations based on data in USDA, ERS, *World Grain*.

28. USDA, ERS, *World Grain*.

29. USDA, ERS, *World Grain*; USDA, ERS, *An Economic Analysis*; USDA, ERS, *World Grain*.

30. USDA, ERS, *World Grain*; Ye. F. Zorina, B. F. Kosov, and S. D. Prokhorova, "The Role of the Human Factor in the Development of the Gullying in the Steppe and Wooded Steppe of the European USSR," *Soviet Geography*, January 1977.

31. Quoted in Vera Rich, "Soil First," *Nature*, February 12, 1982.

32. Jiang Degi et al., "Soil Erosion and Conservation in the Wuding River Valley" (Beijing: Yellow River Conservancy Commission, April 1980), cited in S.A. El-Swaify and E.W. Dangler, "Rainfall Erosion in the Tropics: A State-of-the-Art," in American Society of Agronomy, *Soil Erosion and Conservation in the Tropics*, ASA Special Publication No. 43 (Madison, Wisconsin: 1982); Josef R. Parrington et al., "Asian Dust: Seasonal Transport to the Hawaiian Islands," *Science*, April 8, 1983.

33. U.S. Agency for International Development, *Fiscal Year 1980 Budget Proposal for Ethiopia*, Washington, D.C., 1978.

34. USDA, ERS, China: *Agriculture and Trade Report*, June 1988; USDA, ERS, China: *Situation and Outlook Report*, July 1986; World Bank, *World Development Report 1988*; USDA, ERS, *World Grain*.

35. Lester R. Brown, "Conserving Soils," in Lester R. Brown et al., *State of the World 1984* (New York: Norton, 1984).

36. Kenneth Newcombe, *An Economic Justification for Rural Afforestation: The Case of Ethiopia*, Energy Department Paper No. 16 (Washington, D.C.: World Bank, 1984); Kenneth Newcombe, "Household Energy Supply: The Energy Crisis That Is Here To Stay!" presented to the World Bank Senior Policy Seminar-Energy, Gabarone, Botswana, March 18–22, 1985.

37. Ibid.

38. Gandhi statement from national broadcast of January 5, 1985, as quoted in Government of India, "Strategies, Structures, Policies: National Wastelands Development Board," New Delhi, mimeographed, February 6, 1986.

39. K. G. Tejwani, Land Use Consultants International, private communication, July 3, 1983; Center for Science and Environment, *The State of India's Environment 1982* (New Delhi: 1982); USDA, ERS, *An Economic Analysis*.

40. Margheim, *Implementing Conservation Compliance.*

41. USDA, FAS, *World Grain;* FAO, *Current World Fertilizer Situation and Outlook 1985/86–1991/92* (Rome: FAO, 1987).

42. Sidy Gaye, "Glaciers of the Desert," *Ambio,* Vol. 16, No. 6, 1987; Asim I. El Moghraby et al., "Desertification in Western Sudan and Strategies for Rehabilitation," *Environmental Conservation,* Autumn 1987; Djibril Diallo, "Saving Timbuktu," *Africa Recovery,* December, 1987.

43. Lester R. Brown, "Conserving Soils," in Lester R. Brown et al., *State of the World 1984* (New York: Norton, 1984).

44. World Bank, *World Development Report 1982* (New York: Oxford University Press, 1982); Sloggett and Dickason, *Ground-Water Mining;* Ashok V. Desai, "The Indian Electric Power System," *Economic and Political Weekly,* October 10, 1987; B. D. Dhawan, "Management of Groundwater Resource: Direct Versus Indirect Regulatory Mechanisms," *Economic and Political Weekly,* September 5–12, 1987.

45. Frederick W. Crook, *Agricultural Statistics of the People's Republic of China, 1949–86* (Washington, D.C.: USDA, ERS, April 1988).

46. Center for Monitoring the Indian Economy, Economic Intelligence Service, *Basic Statistics Relating to the Indian Economy, Vol. 1: All India* (Bombay: 1984).

47. FAO, *FAO Production Yearbook 1986* (Rome: 1986); Sloggett and Dickason, *Ground-Water Mining;* Sandra Postel, *Water: Rethinking Management in an Age of Scarcity,* Worldwatch Paper 62 (Washington, D.C.: Worldwatch Institute, December 1984).

48. *FAO Production Yearbook,* various years; USDA, ERS, *USSR: Agriculture and Trade Report,* Washington, D.C., May 1988.

49. David Fraser, "Water Crisis Threatens to Dry Up China's Future," *New Straits Times,* May 8, 1986; Postel, *Water: Rethinking Management;* Sloggett and Dickason, *Ground-Water Mining.*

50. Chinese irrigated area fell from 45 million hectares in 1977 to 40 million hectares in 1985, according to data in Crook, *Agricultural Statistics;* Li Rongxia, "Irrigation System in Central Shaanxi," *Beijing Review,* December 14–20, 1987; Nie Lisheng, "State Organizes Farmers to Work on Irrigation," *China Daily,* January 16, 1988.

51. Sloggett and Dickason, *Ground-Water Mining.*

52. David Fraser, "Water Crisis Threatens to Dry Up China's Future," *New*

Straits Times, May 8, 1986; Postel, *Water: Rethinking Management*; Sloggett and Dickason, *Ground-Water Mining*.

53. Salamat Ali, "Adrift in Flood and Drought," *Far Eastern Economic Review*, August 27, 1987; Navin C. Joshi, "Ground Water Crisis Swells Up," *Business Standard*, April 26, 1988; B. B. Vohra, *When Minor Becomes Major: Some Problems of Ground Water Management* (New Delhi: Advisory Board on Energy, December 1986).

54. Martin Walker, "Sea Turning Into Desert," *Manchester Guardian Weekly*, April 24, 1988.

55. Ibid.

56. Ibid.

57. V. A. Kovda, "Loss of Productive Land Due to Salinization," *Ambio*, Vol. 12, No. 2, 1983.

58. Personal observation by the author.

59. "Farmers Turn Down the Irrigation Tap"; Crook, *Agricultural Statistics*.

60. USDA, FAS, *World Grain Situation and Outlook*, August 1988.

61. Elliot Berg, "Fertilizer Subsidies" (draft), World Bank, Washington, D.C., December 1985.

62. FAO, *FAO Fertilizer Yearbook* (Rome: various years).

63. Anthony M. Tang and Bruce Stone, *Food Production in the People's Republic of China* (Washington, D.C.: International Food Policy Research Institute, May 1980); *FAO Fertilizer Yearbook*, various years.

64. Tang and Stone, *Food Production*.

65. USDA, ERS, *World Grain*; Duane Chapman and Randy Barker, *Resource Depletion, Agricultural Research, and Development* (Ithaca, New York: Cornell University, May 1987).

66. Ibid.

67. Ibid.

68. Robert W. Herdt, *Technological Potential for Increasing Crop Productivity in Developing Countries*, paper presented to the meeting of the International Trade Research Consortium, December 14–18, 1986.

69. Lester R. Brown with Erik P. Eckholm, *By Bread Alone* (New York: Praeger Publishers, 1974); Chapman and Barker, *Resource Depletion*; FAO, *Current World Fertilizer Situation and Outlook*.

70. USDA, ERS, *World Grain*.

71. Hansen, *The Greenhouse Effect*.

72. Quoted in Michael Weisskopf, "'Greenhouse Effect' Fueling Policy Makers," *Washington Post*, August 15, 1988.

73. Hansen, *The Greenhouse Effect*; Manabe, *Climate Warming*; J. Hansen et al., "Global Climate Changes as Forecast by the GISS 3-D Model," *Journal of Geophysical Research*, August 1988.

74. Ibid.; USDA, ERS, *World Grain*.

75. Hansen, *The Greenhouse Effect*.

76. Edward A. Gargan, "Flash Floods and Drought Ravage China," *New York Times*, August 3, 1988; Noel Fletcher, "China's Drought Boosting Food-Import Needs," *Journal of Commerce*, July 25, 1988; "Killing Heat Wave Hits South China," *Beijing Review*, July 25–31, 1988; numerous articles on the drought in *China Daily*, summer 1988; S. Manabe and R. T. Wetherald, "Reduction in Summer Soil Wetness Induced by an Increase in Atmospheric Carbon Dioxide," *Science*, May 2, 1986; Hansen et al., "Global Climate Changes."

77. Sandra Postel, "Stabilizing Chemical Cycles," in Lester R. Brown et al., *State of the World 1987* (New York: Norton, 1987).

78. USDA, NASS, *Crop Production*, August 1988.

79. Hansen, *The Greenhouse Effect*.

80. Ibid.

81. USDA, ERS, *World Grain*.

82. Ibid.

83. World cropland area figure from USDA, ERS, *World Grain*.

84. USDA, FAS, *World Grain Situation and Outlook*, August 1988; data on grain exports from USDA, FAS, *World Grain Situation and Outlook*, August 1988; data on oil exports from British Petroleum Company, *BP Statistical Review of World Energy* (London: June 1987).

85. Urban and Rose, *World Population*.

86. M. Rupert Cutler, "The Peril of Vanishing Farmlands," *New York Times*, July 1, 1980.

87. Organization for Economic Cooperation and Development, *Land Use Policies and Agriculture* (Paris: 1976).

88. Norman A. Berg, "Making the Most of the New Soil Conservation Initiatives," *Journal of Soil and Water Conservation*, January/February 1987.

89. Sandra Postel, *Conserving Water: The Untapped Alternative*, Worldwatch Paper 67 (Washington, D.C.: Worldwatch Institute, September 1985).

90. Yue-Man Yeung, "Urban Agriculture in Asia," (The Food Energy Nexus Programme of the United Nations University, Tokyo, September 1985).

91. J. Dawson Anhalt, "Argentine Agriculture Struggles With Policy Changes," *Choices*, First Quarter 1988; Gary Lee, "Soviets Allow Land Leasing for Farmers," *Washington Post*, August 27, 1988.

92. Erik Eckholm, *The Dispossessed of the Earth: Land Reform and Sustainable Development*, Worldwatch Paper 30 (Washington, D.C.: Worldwatch Institute, June 1979).

93. Population Information Program, "Population and Birth Planning in the People's Republic of China," *Population Reports*, Series J, No. 25, Johns Hopkins University, Baltimore, Maryland, January/February 1982; USDA, ERS, *World Grain*.

LESTER R. BROWN is President and Senior Researcher with the Worldwatch Institute and Project Director of the Institute's annual *State of the World* reports. Formerly Administrator of the International Agricultural Development Service of the U.S. Department of Agriculture, he is author of several books, including *World Without Borders, By Bread Alone, The Twenty-Ninth Day*, and *Building a Sustainable Society*.

THE WORLDWATCH PAPER SERIES

*Worldwatch Papers 2, 4, 5, 6, 8, 9, 11, 12, 13, 14, 15, 17, 19, 20, 22, 23, 24, 26, 27, 32, and 37 are out of print.

Bulk Copies (any combination of titles)   **Single Copy** $4.00
    2–5: $3.00 each   6–20: $2.00 each   21 or more: $1.00 each

Calendar Year Subscription (1988 subscription begins with Paper 81)   U.S. $25.00 _____

Make check payable to Worldwatch Institute
1776 Massachusetts Avenue, NW, Washington, D.C. 20036 USA

Enclosed is my check for U.S. $ _____

_____
name
_____
address
_____
city   **state**   **zip/country**

four dollars

Worldwatch Institute
1776 Massachusetts Avenue, N.W.
Washington, D.C. 20036 USA